Stay with Us

Translated by John Drury

STAY WITH US

François Chagneau

NEWMAN PRESS

New York Paramus, N.J. Toronto

A Newman Press Edition, originally published under the title *Reste avec nous* by Desclee & Cie, Tournai, Belgium, copyright © 1969.

Library of Congress
Catalog Card Number: 70-152311

Design by Nancy Dale Muldoon

Cover Photo by Will Faller

Published by Newman Press
Editorial Office:
304 W. 58th St., N.Y., N.Y. 10019
Business Office:
400 Sette Drive, Paramus, N.J. 07652

Printed and bound in the
United States of America

PREFACE

Any process of renewal contains a certain element of crisis within it, and the renewal that has been taking place in the Catholic Church over the past few years is no exception. However, while the Church is living through a period of crisis, we should not overdramatize this fact inasmuch as this is a condition accompanying any authentic process of renovation.

One of the areas where this crisis is real, if not spectacular, is the prayer life of Christians. They feel ill at ease with the forms bequeathed to them by recent tradition. They also feel ill at ease with most of the forms offered to them by the liturgical renewal—a renewal that had not been adequately assimilated by those who, by virtue of their ministry, should have been its principal artisans. But they may well feel most ill at ease when they break away from pre-established forms and try to pray on their own—either alone or in common. It is not just their forms of prayer that are suspect; it is their very reason for praying. Dissatisfied with forms that seem to be out of date and often incapable of creating new ones, many Christians are gradually getting used to the idea of not praying at all.

This surely cannot be the end result of authentic Church renewal. The revision of forms surely is not meant to bring about the disintegration of content. On the contrary, it should bring out all its relevance and topicality; it should flesh it out for today. But if we are to recover the reality of this domain in all its power and purity, we must do what has to be done in every area: we must follow through on the process we have started, carrying out our quest for truth and authenticity to the very end.

We are undoubtedly beyond the days of using a prayer that was magical to a greater or lesser extent, whereby we hoped to gain some hold on God's will. We are undoubtedly beyond the days of using a prayer that was more or less pagan, whose merit was judged in terms of quantity. We are undoubtedly beyond the days of using a prayer that was more or less pharisaical, whereby we paraded before other people and ensured our status in the community.

There is every reason to rejoice if the day of a new type of prayer has dawned. I now pray to be something more than I am, and to become more truly what God's plan would have me be. The words and gestures and pauses of prayer now help me to take cognizance of what I am in the divine mystery revealed in Jesus Christ. Prayer helps to reveal to me and my conscience the secret relationships to Father, Spirit and all men that are part of my belonging to Christ.

There is every reason to rejoice if the day has come to pray as a Church, to pray with our brothers, to tell ourselves and each other once again about the life of the People of God to which God summons us, so that he may reassemble humanity, now dispersed and divided, into the unity of his well-beloved Son.

I must proclaim my faith in order to live it. I must proclaim my hope in order to affirm it. I must proclaim my love in order to nourish it. I must proclaim my ecclesial life in order to make it a reality. My Christian life needs prayer if it is to grow and flourish. Hopefully the prayers presented here, with their modest aims, will help us to do this.

Bernard Besret

INTRODUCTION

SOME PRACTICAL RECOMMENDATIONS

This book presents six series of texts:

1. Prayers and Reflections (on God, the mystery of Christ, salvation history, etc.).
2. Psalms. Their form and sometimes their content are inspired by those of the Old Testament, and they make use of psalmodic prayer forms.
3. Prayers of Thanksgiving. Each one can be used for different feasts of the liturgical year, or at different times that the user may wish to do so.
4. Short Prayers.
5. Prayers for the Eucharistic Banquet.
6. Sample Office (four readings).

Here it seems advisable to explain the spirit underlying the creation of these texts, and then to explain how each series of texts might be used.

There are two basic approaches to prayer. The first is that of the individual who prays in the privacy of his room. The second is that of a community, be it religious or parochial, large or small. Such a community is by no means a mere juxtaposition of individuals who happen to come together at a given moment to satisfy some legal obligation of a spiritual nature.

The Christian individual needs to be able to express his relationship to God in a form that is personal for him. The Christian people needs to express the fact of its journey toward God in communion with Jesus Christ without being obliged to use formulas that are rigid and somewhat magical, and that are imposed as the only possible forms of expression.

That is why I feel that texts which reflect the quest of one single man ought to be used with full freedom, so that they can dovetail with the prayer of other people. The way to use them, as proposed here, represents a middle ground: between a rigid prayer structure of an obligatory nature, and a total absence of form that leaves everything to individual whim.

If these texts are used in a flexible way, they will hopefully enable people to voice their personal or communal prayer.

PRAYERS AND REFLECTIONS

People are quite free to use these as they wish. They are set up so that the reader can inject his own personal rhythm and add various shadings to the phrases. Using the same words with the same general connotation, he can thus give expression to his varying spiritual moods. It is up to him to find his own form of expression: choosing moments for silence; proclaiming the words or reciting them in a common community pitch; allowing for the recitation of responses; focusing on only one or two parts of the text; prompting the spontaneous reflections of those participating in the Office, etc. In short, the texts can be used in an infinite variety of ways.

PSALMS

This section is not a patchwork quilt of Old Testament psalms. The ones presented here contain both a traditional aspect and one that is hopefully new. The traditional aspect is the spirit of man, which remains fundamentally the same in every age and place. Man explores himself and others, seeks the meaning of life, and experiences moods of sadness, anxiety, joy and confidence.

We do not propose here to add anything new to this aspect of man. Instead, using the approach of the Old Testament psalmist, we hope to express what it means to be Christians since God's revelation in Jesus Christ. When Christ came to fulfill the promises of the Old Testament, he rendered certain themes obsolete: e.g., hatred for one's enemies and God's vengeance. Such themes are not presented here. The themes presented in this book are inspired by the Gospel, insofar as we could manage this. They can be used and recited in different ways. Two choirs may chant the verses alternately or read them verse by verse, or a soloist may chant the verses while the assembly picks up the refrain.

PRAYERS OF THANKSGIVING

These can be recited at the beginning or end of an Office, or somewhere during its course. Here again the user may choose the most suitable procedure, adapting these prayers to the type of office selected and ensuring that they aptly express the prayer of the assembled group.

SHORT PRAYERS

The reader will note that these prayers are brief and have no conclusion. They are brief because the author wanted to express a single idea in one phrase, using a limited number of words. Originally I had tried to create some concluding phrases, but their pastoral implementation proved to be extremely difficult.

Our prayer assemblies have been accustomed to the concluding formula "forever and ever," which evokes the final "Amen." The absence of this formula in most of my new conclusions failed to elicit "Amen" from the group at the proper time. A unanimous "Amen" from the assembly seems more necessary than the systematic use of new concluding phrases without prior instruction and preparation. The most desirable course seems to be for each person to create new concluding formulas that will be in harmony with his community. They should be brief, and they should elicit a concluding "Amen" from the whole assembly.

PRAYERS FOR THE EUCHARISTIC MEAL

These schematic prayers, as one can readily see, follow the classic patterns.

SAMPLE OFFICE

Here the manner of creation and use is more precise. An Office is built around a coherent text based on the Gospel or some chosen theme woven of several texts. The reading of these texts, which develop the same idea or subject, takes place in several stages. Each stage corresponds to the developing thrust of the words or subject theme.

In terms of the assembly, each stage has a moment of silence followed by a résumé of the text. The résumé is chanted alternately by the assembly (the Refrain) and one or more soloists (the Versicle). The moments of silence and of recitation can be spaced differently. As for the lector or lectors, the main thing is that nothing should disrupt the depth and coherence of the Office or engender a monologue that prevents the participants from penetrating the meaning of the text.

CONTENTS

Prayers and Reflections

STAY WITH US, LORD

Stay with us, Lord;
We beg of you
That your path
Remain our path.
We need to have you there.
For we live by your presence
And we are what you are.
It is you alone who are
All that we seek
Obscurely in our dark night.
It is you who are the force
That gives to our struggle
The certain victory of love.

Stay with us, Lord,
And do not go far away.
We are still so close
To that unique moment
When we encountered you,
When you seemed to wait up for us
As we searched for you.
You have not told us everything,
And we would like so much
To know you better,
To profit from your presence
And enjoy your peace.
If you go away again,
Then we must once more start
The never-ending quest
That springs from our emptiness.

Stay with us, Lord,
For in your words we find
All that we are seeking,
All that frees us from ourselves.
When you are there,
So close to us,
Our frailty becomes strength,
And nothing is more precious to us
Than our wretchedness.

Stay with us a little longer
On our journey through this life.
You have the relish of eternity,
And we would not know where to turn
If you were not by our side.
Teach us once again
To be a little more like you.
And then tell us again
What we have not understood:
That you have encountered all mankind,
That they encounter us through you,
And that we stand amid them
As the locus of your presence.

Stay with us, Lord,
For day by day
Time grows late for us.

GOD IN OUR FLESH

I praise and exalt your name
Above all the universe,
Above the earth and sky,
Above the celestial worlds,
Above the realm of living things.

Light of lights to him
Who looks within himself,
I bless and exalt your name.
Christ our very God,
God and Son of God,
Man and brother of men,
Jesus Christ our Lord.

You express for us
Man above all men,
The Being among beings,
The one and only God
Who manifests his love
And invites us to manifest you.
You are the incarnate sign
Who makes our flesh less carnal,
The very Spirit of God
Who molds our earthly clay.

Blessed be our Christ
Who gives us domination
Over every creature.
Blessed be our Christ
For this universe,
Where our encounter is made manifest
And we share your divine being.

Praise to you, O Christ,
For all that you truly are:
God of created time
For centuries unending
As we grow to fullness.
Amen!

ALIVE IN CHRIST

We praise you, God our Father,
For the resurrection of your Son,
For the singular testimony we receive
From this return to life.
We thank you for the light of Easter
And its victory over death.
For now we truly know
That your Son remains with us,
Beyond all time and space,
Beyond all earthly men
And in the life of human beings.

We thank you for putting in our hearts
An understanding of this resurrection
Which ushers us more deeply
Into knowledge of your mystery.
The resurrection of our Jesus
Gives guarantee of life to our love,
Beyond the obstacles of our frail flesh.
Through his death and resurrection,
He frees us from our fetters
And turns us back to you.
And at the very same time
He gives our life its meaning:
The unfolding of a singular love.

He gives our death its purpose,
Its only solid meaning:
Liberation and detachment.
The final step ahead is
The encounter with your life,
The happy vision of your glory
And eternal participation
In light and peace and truth.

OUR PRAYERS FOR THE CHURCH

Lord our God,
We voice our prayers to you
For the Church of Christ, your Son,
For our own Church.
Made up of men who seek your truth,
It can only find
The full measure of faith
If you send your Spirit.

As the image of Jesus Christ
In our humanity,
It contains as well
The burden of our human reality.

It is the Church of Christ
Groping for the road to truth
And a full expression of the faith.
It is the same Church where men,
In the name of Christ,
May impose their ideas,
Coerce human beings
And repress freedom.
It is the same Church where men
See suffering around them,
And offer help but not enough,
And even create further suffering.
It is the same Church
In which men live and struggle
To take on a closer likeness to your Son.

It is the same Church
That knows its imperfections
Yet proclaims to all the world
That you are God.
This Church of ours at times
Knows how to voice your love
And speak to men of the freedom
Which was won by Jesus Christ.

It can be generous
And truly witness to your love.
It can be your life among men
If you breathe your Spirit into it.

That is why, O Lord,
We join together here
And offer prayer to you.

WHO ARE YOU, MY GOD?

Who are you, God that I call mine,
My God?
Who are you, God and Son of my God,
You whom I call Christ?

On what horizon beyond the sea,
In what recess of the earth
Is your name inscribed?
In what unknown being
Shall I find you on my way—
You whom I glimpse perhaps
In the motion of a thought
and the uplift of my spirit?

You I have never seen,
Yet in you I believe and hope,
I who do not know your name.

You slip between my fingers
Like grains of sunlit sand.
You fade away and dissolve
Like snow in the gathering darkness.
When the sun begins to set
And all things fade into the peace of night,
Perhaps then we find your kingdom
As darkness cries out for your light.

At the rising of mankind
You surely did pass on
Life into my numbness
Which I constantly regain.
My whole life seeks for you
And my eye looks for you.

Who are you, God,
You that I believe to be my God,
Christ whom I believe to be Lord,
God of love in whom I hope?

WORDS

We pray to you, God our Father,
With these few words.
And as we pronounce them
We feel in our hearts
The anguish of this void
Which never replies.

Our word is a patchwork of trifles;
It scatters on the wind
Like a cloud of dust.
We know it is needless
For you who every moment
Possess and know us.

God! We utter this name
In a bottomless abyss,
In a void we do not know.
It disappears without returning,
Without ever taking on a sensible form
That our eyes might gaze upon.
Only our human ears
Hear the words of our prayer.
They are sounded and resounded
A thousand times over.
The echo is faithful
But it does not transform them
Or render them answer.
The more we cry out,
The more shape to the echo
Proclaiming your absence
From our seeing eye.

All this we know
And yet we keep praying,
For we have need of it—
Words you have given us
To express ourselves to others
And to express ourselves to you.
Without them everything would wither.
Your love would be vain,

Lost vaguely within us
In the night of our being
And the obscurity of our shadows.

I speak to you, God,
And you do not reply to me.
But the impulse of faith
That dwells within
Assures me that my word
Directed to you
Is an expression of you.

Give us your Word
And let us become it
In the heavy silence of our humanity.
That is why we pray to you,
God our Father.

TURNED TOWARD GOD

We must bless you,
Lord our God,
When nothing that happens
In our life
Brings us toward you.
We must praise you
When we do not understand
And are overcome
By what you send.
We must accept
As coming from you
That which seems without reason or sense
And that which totally escapes our mind.

We must pray to you
Whom we do not know.
We must love you
Whom we do not see.
Who of us can see you?
Who of us does know you?
We can only see or touch
The things that are around us here.
We know the limitations
Of things and men and us ourselves.
How incapable we are
Of acting less like men
To be a little more like you.

It is you who speak to us
In all the happenings of life.
And we are human beings
Who try to understand,
And when we understand
We try to give our answer.
Your dimensions, God,
Escape our formulas.
When we are touched by your love
And animated by your Spirit,
We cannot explain to others

What we glimpse of you.
You are not imprisoned in our spirits.
You are freer than our freedom
Which weighs so heavy at such moments.
How we wish that in one stroke
You would lead all mankind
Into the light of faith
And the communion of your love.

YOU HAVE GIVEN US EVERYTHING

You who know us, Lord,
Who hold us and sound our hearts,
Who see how we are beaten down and broken—
Our spirit no longer comprehends
And knows not where to find you.
For nothing is simple in our life
And our choices are difficult.
I choose you, you the Lord,
But who are you that I speak to?

There is nothing that exists,
Nothing that we choose
Which can halt our endless quest
And give us satisfaction.

Nothing belongs to us alone,
For we possess everything
And you have given it to us:
Good and evil,
Life and death,
Love and hate.
There is where you are to be found.
There is where we must look for you.

What is the good that we must choose
That hides no trace of evil?
Where is the life that we can truly build
That will not lead us into death?
A simple word or thought of ours
Can turn our powers of love
Into tools of hate and destruction.

Come to our aid, O God.
Unveil your face
And reveal your countenance.
Where are you, God,
That we may come to you?

TURN AWAY YOUR FACE

For one moment, Lord,
Turn your face from us.
Take away your light
That we may not see
Your demands.
Then at last we will be able
To be borne up by our own weight
And to live by our own whim.
In the immensity of your absence
You are sometimes all too present
And you weigh upon us.
Our frailty grows weary from your power.
It would like to live on its own,
To gain thereby a little strength.

The love that you give us
And demand of us
Is often too broad and full of life.
It stifles us
Because it does not give us a chance
To breathe on our own.
Your freedom weighs down upon our shoulders.
And your truth,
Which transports us outside ourselves,
Is sometimes a painful thing to live
And difficult to witness to.
We are still so attached to this our earth
That we cannot bear more of you.

And yet, Lord, should you disappear,
This solid earth would gape beneath our feet.
Our life, however full of weight,
Would lose its sense and purpose.
Only you, Lord, can transform us,
Can turn our life into that of your Son,
Can fortify our frailty with your strength,
That is why as humble men
Can make us over into you completely.
In all the poverty of our means
We offer prayer to you, O Lord.

DEATH

Lord our God,
It is at the end of our life
That our understanding fails us,
When we touch the core of our humanity
And cease to journey with you.
Our death is a reality
That we do not accept.
It is imposed upon us
And leaves us sad,
Opening our eyes
To contemplate the abyss.
It seems to be so alien to you
In its brutal inexorability.

How are we to realize
That this inevitable finale
Is the beginning of something else
In the continuing course of life?
How can we acknowledge that this disintegration
Is a time of unity?
For a space of troubled years
We have worked in the fire of your love
To make ourselves what we are,
To create new life and build up humanity,
To lead man to his fuller flowering.
How can we acknowledge and accept
That all this ends in an instant?
How can we accept
That the hour of our death
Is the time for a greater encounter
With the one and only real love?
How can we manage to say,
In these difficult moments
When our earthly matter
Treads its way through life,
That death is in service to life,
That it is the gateway
From limited life
To the fullness of life?
You alone are the answer,

O Lord, to our anguish.
Only through your Spirit
Does this final detachment
Take on meaning for us
As the moment when everything
Is offered to us.

FAITH

Lord, we pray,
Give increase to our faith.
Bring it to full flower
And to its only true fulfillment:
Which is sharing in your light
And living in your peace.

Give to our faith
The strength of certitude in your love.
Let it receive from your Spirit
The quickening impulse of hope.
Bestowed on us by you
And animated by this hope,
May our faith light up our lives
And let them truly share
In man's salvation history.

Do not let our faith
Become a static thing,
A lifeless personal possession.
Let it be the start
Of our continuing quest,
Pressing eagerly forward
To discover your truth and wisdom.
May this faith that strives for you
Permeate our lives
Vivifying and transforming them
Into a gift of love.

You alone, our God,
Can guard this faith for us.
You alone can keep us ever aware
Of what you have offered to all men,
Reminding us that your gift
Summons us to respond with greater love,
A love that will work through us and beyond us
To gather all our brothers
Into the unity of your light and peace.

WHAT HAS HAPPENED TO YOUR LOVE

You, God, are the source of all things.
You have created love, or, better yet,
You have not created it
Because love is you yourself.
It is your being and your person,
Everything that you are.
And what is more, God,
You have given this love
A singular human countenance
Of flesh and blood.
In our flesh and blood
It reveals its power and truth.
So if love is truly you
And if this face of love is you as well,
You, our God and Lord,
With good reason we may ask
What we have done and still do every day
To the love that mirrors you
And was given by your Son.

Your love is the source of life.
What has happened to that life?
Your love means sharing,
And what do we do about sharing?
Your love is giving,
And who of us gives himself?
Your love is light,
So why this darkness?
Your love means true fulfillment;
What has happened to your creatures?
Your love is unity;
Why such disunity?

The love we live
Is an empty word
That rings emptily
Through your universe.
It is a source of hate

And deep misunderstanding
That carries with it death.
It burns without giving warmth,
Seizing only to destroy.
Nothing is truly given
Without hope of some return.
People who say they love
Love only for themselves,
Expecting that they can give
Without being separated from themselves.
Man's love is secret, shadowy, sinuous
And totally distant from your light.

What has become of your countenance
And where does your name lie lost?
Do you recognize your Son
Deformed and crucified every day?
What has happened to your love?
What has become of you?
Who are you, God?

UNITY

What is man, O Lord,
And who is he?
Can one truly recognize him
In his bewildered countenance
And senseless agitation?
Do you recognize him,
This work of your own hands?
You know from where he comes,
But do you also know
Where he is heading now
Through rancor and indifference?

He is capable of so much love
And equally of hate.
He can work in obstinate effort
To build his dream in hard-earned sweat,
To labor blindly for the pleasure of success.
But he can also find his pleasure
In a gesture of destruction
That eventually destroys himself.
He thirsts and hungers for eternity,
Without being able to satisfy desire,
Often taking the opposite road
Than that which leads to peace.

Mindful of unity,
It is the thing he seeks in life.
But he would hope to find it
By dividing himself from self,
Dividing others around him
And opposing himself to them.

He is capable of finding self-fulfillment
In the fulfillment of another.
He can patiently wait upon another
And do all things for a smile of love,
Finding there his further growth.
But he can also turn away
And wound the person
Who loves him.

Lord, recognize this human being
Who tries at times
To stammer out your name,
Who raises his arms to you
In a gesture of expectation.

Lord, we pray you,
In our unrest
Be the response
We truly need.

IN MY SOLITUDE

I am alone
On the road I travel,
On the road you take me,
Drawing me on with a force
That exceeds all human demands.

I am alone
And I feel this solitude
Like a deeply open wound
In the depths of my being.
All those who surround me
Are only shadowy figures,
Vanishing furtively
At the sound of my appeal.
They flee and disappear
When I try to approach them.

And the time is coming
When I will settle into this solitude
And it will be my lone companion.

I do not know from where
This solitude comes to me.
Does it come from you?
Is it the only road
Where I will discover you
And find at last your truth?
Or does it come from other men
Who refuse to give me love
And thus drive me deeper down
Into a life of cold indifference?
Or does it come from me,
Repulsing other human beings
As I try to draw them to me?

I walk, O Lord, in solitude
And the silence resounds in my ears
More loudly than the shouts of men.
I walk, O Lord, in solitude,
Plunging deeper into it
As I journey on to you,
My Lord and God.

FINDING GOD AGAIN

God of mercy,
You express yourself in the discovery of man.
But how shall we find you again
There where we feel your absence?
How shall we find you again
Behind the visage of shame
That covers our faces?
How shall we find you now
When the brotherly love
We thought to live humbly day by day
Has neither force nor purity nor truth?
When our brother men and we
Hide your heavenly light,
How can we find you?

Everything is now deformed
By the way we live.
No longer is it your light.
Your light is strong and radiant,
Ours is pale and weak.
Your light is straight and forthright,
Ours vacillates with us.
We believe in the words
Uttered by the tongue
That you have given us;
But they are no longer your Word.
Your Word is life-giving,
Our words bring death.
Your Word is truth,
Our lips proclaim a lie.
And to all that, O Lord,
We give your name,
Proclaiming your paternity.
We think we possess your Spirit
But we have the spirit of the world.
We speak lies and cowardly things,
Hypocrisy and base compromise.
We proclaim the message of death.
Has Jesus Christ been realized
In our brothers?

I look around me everywhere,
Scanning the faces of other men
For the visage of your Son.
But I see only wretched frailty
Reflecting my own sins.

God of mercy and our hope,
When fulfillment will be reached
In these men of flesh and blood
Through you who can transform all things,
We believe that Jesus Christ
Will pass into our humanity.

LEAD US INTO THE DESERT

Lead us through the desert,
Lord.
Its power and barrenness
And immense oppression
Proclaim your name to our ears.

May we be like the desert
Imbibing your true Word.
May it envelop our lives
Like the forceful gust of wind
That flows from the infinite.

May your breath pick us up
Like so many grains of sand
Gathered from the corners of the earth.

Lead us to your desert.
May we discover there,
In the depths of our own selves,
In the truth of emptiness
And the purity of absence,
That you are present Lord.

May we become this desert.
May the deep abyss of our being
Be a summons to your name.
May we become this name
Lost in the infinite horizon
Of your desert,
You, our God!

EVERYTHING SPEAKS OF GOD

Lord, our God and Father,
Everything here below,
Everything here around us,
Speaks to us of you:
Everything that strikes our eyes,
Our hands, our bodies, and our lives.
All is sunlight that speaks your name,
For it is in your image,
Light and heat for us.
And you are all.
Light and heat and everything here
In a flash springs into life
When it turns toward you.

In our lowly sky
Coated now with gray
We find you, the Lord.
You stretch out beyond the horizon
Where our eye gets lost in viewing.
You are more unfathomable
Than the gray of this our sky.
You are more an absolute
Than the sky that covers our earth.

And your human creatures, God,
Speak your name to us.
In their very life they are
The witness to your life.
You are more profound
Than any glance can be.
You give life to us
More than the breath
That stirs within us.
And the lips that you fashioned in love
Can acknowledge you by name.

For this earth so solid
Where we spend our lives,
We praise you as our God.
For the life you give

To all that now surrounds us,
We bless you as our God.
For giving us a chance
To see, admire, search, discover,
We thank you as our God.
For our eyes and hands and bodies,
For all the earth and sky,
For all that you are,
We praise you, Lord our God.

YOU ARE THERE

God, you do not speak
In the language of men
And you do not dialogue with us.
Your life
Is not our life
And your love is not our love.
Our knowledge
That you wish to be solid and rich
Is far from your wisdom.
The earth where we live,
Where we try to live,
Is not the only place
Where you might exist.

And yet
We know that you are there,
That you offer yourself
Through everything that we live.
Your name is in our speech
And our lips do praise you.
A man in our midst
Using human words
Has told us of you.

GOD IS DISTANT AND NEAR

Our life is too short
And our words are too feeble
To tell you our thoughts
And live out your love.
You are so far distant from us
And so immensely great,
Residing above this earth and us.
Nothing of ours could reach you
If you did not come to us.
You are the infinite and the inaccessible
Above all else.

Nothing is greater than you
Who have yourself so small.
Nothing is more distant than you
Who have brought yourself so near.
We see you everywhere around us:
In human beings,
Their looks, their work,
The air they breathe.
It is through them that you come to us,
And you enter our lives to approach them.

In their frailty and power,
In the whole course of their lives,
We discover ourselves.
We are summoned by your love
To reveal your life to them.
We are drawn by your power
To proclaim to them your salvation.

YOU ARE EVERYWHERE

God, you are everywhere.
You are in the place and time
That we pronounce your name.
We have freely accepted
The choice that you have made of us
And that you continue to make
All the days of our lives.
We accept what we have learned of you
From Jesus Christ, your Son.
You are everywhere and always.
You are for all times.
And when we speak of you,
You use our lips
To be proclaimed to all creation.

GOD'S GLANCE

Lord, you see us before you,
Trembling or filled with confidence,
United or torn asunder.
We bear our humanity in our hands
Stretched toward you,
In the hands that fashion you
By their toil.

We are not concerned to know
Who you are or how you exist,
The why and wherefore
Of all that surrounds us.
We are not concerned to find
The traces of your power and glory.

We are content to know
That we are there,
Living in our flesh and blood,
And loving through them,
And straining toward you.

We are content to know
That you are there
And that you see us.
Your glance we do not meet.
It is not brightened by joy
Or darkened by sadness.
But it is everything
Because it is creative.
It gives us plenitude
Because it is a glance of love.

LIVING IN GOD

We need only pray to you
To bear up in our hearts,
In the weight of a single thought,
The whole mystery that makes us men.
We are a wondrous and unique arrangement
Of might and frailty,
Of love and hate,
Of grandeur and poverty.

We need only have your Spirit
To understand our humanity,
To know that in mankind
We find your love and truth,
Your salvation and liberty.

In you each man finds his place,
In you he grows to be a creator.
All our frailty calls out for your power
And your power is etched in it.
Your singular love is the answer
To our divisiveness,
The response of your perfection
To the question that is life.

Your creation bears in us
A choice for grandeur
And the expression of your name
In total liberty.
There is no poverty
That is not wealth in your glance.
And we can only choose you
By responding to your choice.
You give us our true meaning,
You give impetus to our life,
You let us experience your love
In Jesus Christ.

WE ARE CREATED DIFFERENT

We give you thanks,
God our Father,
For having created us
Each different from the other.
Our faces radiate every color
And your light plays over their variety.
We thank you for having given us
A variety of languages,
Thus varying our quest for you
In human forms of expression.
My brother is different from me
And it is very good that way.
In this difference is imbedded
All our richness.
My approach to him
Will be more difficult
But also more exalting.
And his approach to me
Will be more filled with care.

We praise you, Lord,
For allowing us
To discover one another
And know the joy of encounter.
You have enabled us
To share ourselves
And thus make an offering.

Above all we give you thanks
Because that which makes us different
Fashions our unity.
With every human language
And every human life
And every fresh stirring of love
We can say that you are God;
We can see that you are gathering us
Into one with Jesus Christ,
Who is one with you and us.

LET US DISCOVER YOU

Let us, O God, discover you
In the world,
Read you in the events
Of our history.
Open our spirits
To the search for your love.
Teach our lips
To pronounce your name.
Teach our hands
To build up your kingdom.

For you are in our quest;
It is you who animate it.
You are in our life;
It is you who give it rhyme and reason—
You, its only true goal.
With a little more love
We can offer your glory
The finest praise.
With a little more joy
We can give your creation
Its true visage: yours.

You are great, O Lord.
You are truly our God.
You give man his true fullness
By exposing him to all your mystery,
By inspiring him to sing
The glory of your name.

MAN'S SOLITUDE

God, your eternity in a single glance
Envelops all the days of man
And every human life
In a gesture of love.
Teach us, we pray,
To understand and love
Our solitude.
May we learn to choose it
Day by day
And help to brighten
The solitude of others.

For it gives roots
To our whole life,
And it pervades our moments,
Detaching us from what is not ourselves.
It permits us to be truly free,
And through it we come to understand
The richness of another.
It itself calls forth encounter with men.

Help us to long for the moment
When this solitude will disappear,
When there will be revealed to us
Your glory.
For there is no longer solitude
When in your life
We possess the whole universe;
When your glance becomes our glance
And your love ours.
Help us to collect our strength
In the power of our solitude.
Let it usher us into the hope
Of being no longer ourselves,
To become totally other.

PRAYER

Lord,
We raise our prayer to you.
Be it a fervent supplication
Or a word of thanksgiving,
It comes from you
And returns to you
In a spirit of encounter
Between our humanity and you.
It marks the discovery of your love
In other men,
The revelation of their life
In your truth,
And an awareness of their mystery
In the power of your love and truth.

Our prayer comes from you,
Because it gathers us together
To unite us in your love,
To be a gesture of love
Drawing us to you.

Our prayer comes from you
And then returns to you.
You alone
Can give it true fulfillment.
You alone
Can go beyond the words
To know our thoughts,
Can get beyond our actions
To know our desires
And animate our lives.

Our prayer comes from you
Even as does your light
Which reveals your countenance,
Even as do our thoughts
Inspired by your Spirit.
It gives us expression
As you keep us moving
Toward our encounter with you.

Even as the light
Descends on darkness,
Even as the rain
Descends on the parched earth,
So your peace
Descends upon our anxiety.

In our prayer you come to us, O Lord,
And through our prayer we go toward you.

INVITATORIES FOR LAUDS

I

Brethren,
God grants us this day
To see once more his light;
He opens our eyes to the creation
That stirs awake as we do.
Let our song and prayer
Tender him our thanks
For renewing life in us.
Through his Holy Spirit
May he lead us today
To the fullness of his love.

II

Brethren,
Light comes to dispel the shadows.
Now that night has passed
Let us join our voices
And turn toward God our Father,
Toward Jesus Christ, his Son,
Who vanquished night and death.
Let us chant our joy
For the day that is reborn
And witness to the life
Of their Holy Spirit.

III

Brethren,
We greet the new day.
May God inspire us
To chant his praises.
After our separation during the night
May he help us to find again
Our communion as brothers.
Let us praise and bless him
With one heart and voice.

IV

Brethren,
The Lord our God,
Creator of the universe
That surrounds us,
Has given us nights for rest
And days for working.
During the night
While darkness still reigned,
He kept us from death and evil.
That is why we desire
In these first hours of daylight
To tender him our praise
And that of all creation
For the grandeur of his name.

V

Brethren,
In these first hours of daylight
When light breaks through the night
Dispelling darkness with its splendor,
Let us praise our God and Father
In oneness of hearts and voices.
For he is the inaccessible light
That brightens up our lives
And illumines all creation.

VI

Brethren,
Let our spirits awaken.
Let us walk in joy and gladness
Toward God our Father.
The sun that is rising with the day
Summons us to remember Jesus Christ.
He is the brightest sun of all,
The light beyond all lights,
Who never sets or sleeps.
Let us praise God for his Son.
Let us praise him for his love.
Let us join with all creation
To offer him our praise.

PENITENTIAL EXERCISE

I

We turn toward you, our Father,
Imploring mercy and pity
For our sins,
For all that separates us from you,
For all that in and through us
Causes men to suffer
And crucifies Christ again.
When we probe our human nature,
We know well that we are sinners.
When we look within ourselves
We see our frailty and wretchedness.
And so we set ourselves before you,
Asking that your infinite love
Will re-enkindle our conversion
Through your Holy Spirit.

II

Lord, behold our dire neediness
And everything that divides us.
In the love we purport to bear
For our human brothers,
We are always seeking
The reflection of our own image.
And when we propose to heed our brothers
In your sacred name,
There persists within us
Another alien intent:
To show ourselves as bright and better,
To prove ourselves the means of succor,
To pose as owners of your pardon and mercy.

III

Although we know
That you alone are truth
And usher us into it,
We try to pretend
That when it comes to us

It stays with us as our possession.
In our delusion we believe
That we do own your truth.
We propose to force this truth on others,
To give them an image of you
That is really ours.
For this terrible misuse of your truth,
Pardon us, O Lord.

IV

We proclaim
That you alone are love,
Creating us by love
And giving us true life
Through Jesus Christ, your Son.
We know that we are called
To live this love of yours.
And reveal it to all men.
But every single day
We take advantage of your love
To make our own life better.
In the name of your love
We use people for our own satisfaction.
We make your love our servant.
For this singular love
Which we distort so meanly,
For this infinite love
Which we drain away,
For this source of life
Which we turn to death,
Pardon us, O Lord.

V

Through your Son, Jesus Christ,
You gave us liberty.
But you did not give it
To just a few of us
Privileged by your love;
Your liberty is poured out
On every human being.
And that we do not accept.

We misuse your liberty
To constrict our brother men,
Begrudging them the chance
To acknowledge you in freedom
As the one and only God.
In freedom's name
We urge upon them
One single way to see and know you,
One single way to live your message.
We think to bring them life, your life,
But that is what we then injure.
For all those that we bind in fetters,
For your Son who is fettered every day,
Pardon us, O Lord.

VI

Through your son, Jesus Christ,
You have given us your light.
Through us it should radiate
With dazzling splendor through the world
As the very revelation
Of your power and salvation.
But we hold it jealously,
Closely guarded within ourselves.
We try to be the only ones
Who see and know you
And benefit from your love.
For your light which we enfeeble,
Pardon us, O Lord.

VII

Through Jesus Christ, your Son,
And the promise he made to us,
You sent to us your Spirit.
He will gather us together,
Forming of our communion
The countenance of your Son
Revealed to all mankind.
But far from being inspired by your Spirit,
Our deeds and words provoke around us
Conflict, division and hatred.
While your Spirit is free and blows where he wills,

We proclaim we are his only expression,
That it cannot possibly be true
That he would inspire others.
For this offense against your Spirit,
Pardon us, O Lord.

VIII

Of all this, Lord, we are aware.
We know that we must every day
Arise again with Christ, your Son
To vanquish our own sins.
We know that your almighty power
Is to pass through our frailty
So that through our poverty
Your glory may be expressed.
When our frailty and poverty
Are transfigured by your Spirit,
We believe that they will lead
To a revelation of your love.

IX

Come down to us, O Lord,
While we are turned to you
In expectation of your mercy.
Enkindle in us a deep desire
For reconciliation with our brothers.
Only you can ensure
That we are pardoned by those
Whom we have offended.
Only you can ensure
That our pardon will go out
To those who offended us.
And we hope and pray
That the wondrous power of your pardon
Will descend on all mankind.

X

Lord, when we are reconciled with our brothers
We see that your love for us
Is embodied in love for our brothers,

And that we express your love to them
Through the power of our own love.
Take away from us everything
Which bespeaks hostility and division,
And help us to proclaim
That you are love,
Truth,
Light,
Liberty.

PRAYER OF INTERCESSION

Lord, hear our prayer,
Pay heed to our words
And penetrate our hearts.
You have inspired in us the love
Which is the source of our prayer.
And with these few brief words
We wish to unite all our brothers
Who more than anyone else have need
Of your Spirit's help.

May only our love be before your eyes,
You who give it all its meaning.

Lord, we pray for those
Who think they are living this love
When they only seek to dominate
And forget to lose themselves,
Who love only when they are receiving
And refuse to give of themselves.
We pray for them, O Lord,
Prisoners of empty words
That have no meaning.
Theirs is a facile love that speaks delusion,
Masking the reality of their solitude.
Grant that they may find the strength to love
By finding themselves in finding others.
May they find in love
Your light and peace.

Lord, we pray for those
Who turn away from love,
The cynical and jaded people
Who never accept the gift of love
That another can offer them.
We pray for these blind people
Who cannot discern the truth,
Who cannot discover the purity
In a smile of love
Or in an act of love,
Who refuse to open up to the life

That can come to them through love.
Lord, open their eyes
To the loving presence
Of those who lose and forget themselves
In the work of love.
May they teach them to give of themselves
By comprehending the gift of others.

Lord, we pray for the unknown ones
Whom no one will ever love
And who will never love anyone;
Who will ever look on love
As a strange and alien realm
Toward which they feel indifferent.
Lord, we pray for those
Who really do love love
Without ever being able to live it.
And also for those who only feel
The pangs of their solitude
Or the suffering of abandonment
When they look from without upon
The love of other human beings,
Developing all around them
Without encompassing them.

Lord, grant that they may be loved,
That they may encounter a love
Which will vitalize their lives
And carry them toward you.

Lord, we pray for those
Who haunt the ways of love,
For those who shed the power of love
On other people without repayment.
For those whose care is answered
By indifference or neglect.
For those who never get to experience
The full fruit of their self-giving
In the response of another.
For those who are able to smile
Without ever seeing a return,
Who offer acts of love
That no one chooses to share.

Lord, take away their weariness
And let their love explode.
May they find among our brothers
Those who will receive in their love
Witness to your life.

Lord, we pray for all our brothers
Whose love is a hidden, secret thing
That cannot unfold in the light of day,
For those whose love is a constraint
Lost and unsatisfied.
Grant that they may find
A place in our society
Where their love can find expression.
Teach them that love is liberty;
Free them from the bonds of fear
And lead them into your peace.

Lord, we pray for those
Who live love only for security;
Who guard it jealously
As a tool of their desire;
Who refuse to be challenged by love
Or be drawn to its higher forms.
For those who have frozen love
At one point in life
And refuse its further movement,
Locking others in the confines
Of routine, joyless, unsatisfied love.

Lord, grant that they may understand
That love moves on unendingly;
That it is a choice at every moment;
That we can only win its fruits
By accepting the risks it entails.

Lord, we pray for those,
Our brothers inspired by the Spirit,
Who truly have lived love
As a genuine act of sharing.
For those who in their love
Have worked to develop man
And renew the face of the earth.

For those who by their love
Have led men to their true fulfillment
In the discovery of your truth.
For those who have fully lived your truth,
Leading men to a knowledge of love,
And who will share your love at last
When the whole universe of man
Has perfected its terrestrial presence.

Lord, grant them fidelity,
The strength to keep on striving
For ever greater detachment.
There they will discover you,
The source of their real love.

Lord, we pray that our human love
Through the work of your Spirit
May truly signify justice,
Proclaiming a truth that has no trace
Of falsehood or base compromise.
We pray above all that it may mean
The liberty to which you call
Those who acknowledge your name.

Psalms

LORD, YOU GIVE US LIFE

I give you thanks, Lord my God,
Because you have given me life;
You came and took me in your hands
From the very depths of time.
R. Lord, you give us life.

It is you who shape our visage,
You who give life to our spirit.
You open our eyes to the light
And your Word suffuses our lives.
R. Lord, you give us life.

You snatch us from the darkness
And then give us your love.
With the light of your Son
You pierced the night of time.
R. Lord, you give us life.

You came down to us here
To share in our lives.
You take on our sorrows
And with us have vanquished death.
R. Lord, you give us life.

You vivify us still,
Your Spirit rules our lives.
Your light is our light,
You are present among us.
R. Lord, you give us life.

Your creation gives you glory.
Through your Son man gives you praise.
They join together in your Spirit
Beyond the days and years of time. Amen!
R. Lord, you give us life.

QUEST

I look for you, my God,
In the corridors of my night;
I look for you in men:
Who will speak to me of you?

I come to the end of my journey;
Earth can no longer answer me;
My weary, tired spirit
Seeks but cannot find you.

My feet cannot move ahead,
They are stuck to the ground.
My body is so heavy
And evil sticks to me.

In you alone will I find hope,
For I know that you are love.
You can save me even now
And free me from myself.

I have looked for you in men;
I have hoped to find you there,
In the shadow of a face
Or the palm of an extended hand.

I can do no more, my God.
My body has no strength.
My spirit is totally weak.
I can only wait for you to come.

For you are our recourse
In the aid of Christ our brother.
Your Spirit leads us to you
As he gathers us in time. Amen!

MAKE US ONE PEOPLE

From all corners of the horizon
I see a crowd of human beings approaching.
They throng together in festive celebration
And my heart resounds with joy.
They are coming to the good news
That gathers us into Jesus Christ.

R. We celebrate your name, O Lord.
You alone give us life.

Their festive joy breaks through the darkness,
They gather to claim their liberty.
It is the liberty you give to all
When you deliver us from sin.
You separate all of us from evil
And bring us together in your love.

R. We celebrate your name, O Lord.
You alone give us life.

In their faces beaming brightly,
In their eyes alive with joy,
I see, my God, that you have won them.
You bring them together in one place,
You form of them a single People,
In their love you establish your kingdom.

R. We celebrate your name, O Lord.
You alone give us life.

There is no longer hate between them,
Divisiveness exists no more;
You our God destroy their bondage
And abolish all dividing lines.
Your light has truly transfigured them,
They come from everywhere to share your name.

R. We celebrate your name, O Lord.
You alone give us life.

The bustling throng passes close to me
With their eager arms outstretched.
They snatch me from my deep despair
And liberate me from all my sins.
My spirit exults with joy and opens out to you.
In them I recognize your Son,
I tread the path of your salvation.

R. We celebrate your name, O Lord.
You alone give us life.

We bless you, God our Father,
Who entered our history.
You are present to us in your Son,
Your Spirit gathers us through the ages.

R. We celebrate your name, O Lord.
You alone give us life.

MY SIN IN YOUR EYES

I no longer want to look around me
Or see myself in the dawning day.
I cannot bear the looks of others
Or face you squarely, O my God.

I have sinned against my brethren's lives.
I have refused to give my love.
I stole from you and snuffed out light.
I crucified your only Son
By rejecting my brother men.

My sin is set before me;
It reappears at every turn.
My faults preoccupy my mind
And cause my soul to wither.

I hear the cries of the multitude,
And sense the hatred of these men.
I see the shaking fists
And their lacerating hands.

Because of too little love
And all my past refusals,
I have helped to destroy peace
And hate has devoured the earth.

I can no longer stand before your face, O God.
I flee from you and fear your wrath.
Faced with the enormity of my sins,
I dare not believe in your mercy still.

What corner of the earth can hide me?
I need a place more secret than me,
Inaccessible to your probing glance
That will hide my wretched frailty.

I moved on endlessly
And searched the ends of the earth.
But there was no one there
To take me in willingly.

Look at me beaten and broken,
With no more tears to shed.
There is no strength left in me;
There is only you, my God!

SONS OF GOD

Happy is the man among us
Who has received his life on earth,
Who has accepted all from God
And journeys in his peace.

> Happier still is he
> Who has received Christ in his brothers;
> He has found true love in them
> And journeys toward the light.

His path is not marred by sidetracks;
His footstep is firm and sure;
Doubt no longer plagues him,
He journeys on with Christ.

> He gets through the bustle of life,
> And bears the storm of anxiety.
> He survives the pangs of hate,
> For he leans upon the Lord.

May all men come together
Uniting in their brother.
May Christ be realized in them
As they walk with him to the Father.

> Glory to you, our divine wisdom,
> To your Son, incarnate love,
> Who gives us now your Spirit
> To gather us into one. Amen!

SUFFERING AND SALVATION

I am afraid, O Lord my God,
When I look ahead before me,
When I open up my spirit
Toward your final trek.

> I see myself in suffering,
> Debased by other men.
> They beat and mock and jeer me
> And lead me gaily to my death.

Tell me, God my refuge,
What have I done to them?
Their flesh and blood are in me,
I have lived their very life.

> Why did they look at me in horror,
> When I offered them but love?
> Why did they raise their fist at me,
> When I came to give them freedom?

I came to bring them joy,
To reveal to them your name,
To have them forget their pains
And hear of your salvation.

> I loved them more than myself;
> I found myself again in their children.
> To those who came to me
> I bore witness of your love.

How harsh your message is for me!
I tremble when I speak of you.
But I know that you are life,
That nothing separates me from you.

> I sing of your glory, Lord,
> I find succor in your strength.
> Your Spirit opens my eyes
> And I see your Son in men. Amen!

GOD REVEALS HIS SALVATION

When my prayer ascends to you,
My soul is seized by doubt,
My spirit trembles and I am afraid:
Who are you, O my Lord?

> I speak to you but you never reply,
> I call out your name to the universe.
> I search throughout the world
> But never find your life.

Speak to me, God my refuge,
Reveal your face to me.
Tell me who you are, show me your light,
Erase my doubt and give me your peace.

* * *

In the dawning orient of earth
I saw a brilliant light.
I saw the darkness scatter
At the coming of your Son.

> I thank you, God my Father,
> For unveiling yourself to me,
> For deigning that your Spirit
> Should let me know your Son.

My fellow men and friends,
Come, let us join together
And raise our voice in song
For him who comes to us.

COME, LORD

The suffering of all mankind
Seeks and summons you through my lips;
It shouts its despair to you
And waits but for your love.

You who know all things,
Look and see us men;
Incline your ear attentively
And take in all our suffering.

Our world is torn and devastated,
War destroys creation.
Cries of sorrow come from everywhere
And anxiety is our daily bread.

The innocent no longer exists,
Dead for some time now.
Hate establishes its kingdom,
And where are you, the Lord?

The throng of countless men
And the shackles of the poor
And the catalog of our miseries
Confront you with pressing questions.

Why is there no food for children?
Why the wretchedness of peoples?
Why these ceaseless devastations?
No one sees you, the Lord.

And yet you are there, O God;
You too are seeking your Son,
Him whom you are to fashion
By uniting the whole universe.

There is always something of Jesus
In a suffering countenance,
In man's unquiet gaze
And all our human anguish.

How hard to bring all men together,
How heavy love is for him to bear!
O God, who can reunite all,
Give ear to our expectation.

You are greater than all our ages,
Your Spirit hovers over men,
Your salvation comes to us through your Son
And your love is for every age. Amen!

WAITING FOR GOD

The Lord our God knows us well
As an author knows his work.
He is at the heart of all our anguish
And in the depths of our hope.

Our memory bears the weight
Of all men's memories;
They come from the depths of time,
Bearing their hopes and pains.

In us the Lord replies,
In us he prepares his return.
He leads us along this earth
To the coming day of his return.

May all men still remember,
And through them may we too,
That God brings us salvation
Through him who is his Son.

The Lord is coming to help us,
He is coming to break our chains;
In the power of his strength
He binds us to his love.

For he is God forever
With Jesus, his only Son;
His Spirit still is with us,
He gathers us through the ages. Amen!

GOD THE CREATOR

Our God is Lord
Over earth and heaven.
Near and far from us
He speaks to us through this earth.

He does not dwell in our dwelling places,
He does not live in our towns.
Nothing serves him like a man,
For he does not live our life.

For it is he who animates us,
He is our life and breath.
In him our earth was created
And he gives all things life.

We all live in quest of him,
And know not where to find him.
Our hands go out in the night
And our spirits seek his name.

Now we know what his name is,
In Jesus Christ we learn it.
God comes toward us in justice,
Raising us among the dead.

Our breath is from God,
Through Jesus Christ we praise him.
It is his Spirit that unites us
And all the peoples of the earth. Amen!

CONVERSION

I was scouring this earth of the Lord,
I was chaining the hands of men,
I was rebelling against love
When the Lord appeared to me.

He overturned my escorts,
He scattered all my friends.
My face was driven to the ground
And a light pierced through my eyes.

From the heavens the Lord addressed me:
Why do you persecute me?
Why do you enslave men?
Why do you bring them death?

And darkness enveloped my countenance,
My glance no longer looked to earth.
Only my heart knew my distress
And my eyes wept from remorse.

The Lord is in the darkness;
All is light before him.
The night is like day to him,
Like a brightly burning fire.

My eyes are open to a new life,
They shine with a stunning splendor.
They see the earth of the Lord
And look with the love of Jesus Christ.

May my darkness accept his light,
May my lips proclaim his name.
All the earth will know of his love
And all men will see his salvation.

Praised be God for the life he gives us,
For his love in Jesus Christ,
For his Spirit that vivifies us
Until the end of time. Amen!

DO NOT ABANDON ME

From the depths of my frailty
And all my wretchedness,
Lord, I beg you, please
Turn your face to me.

I am swallowed up in anguish
And I touch my very depths.
My life is now for nought
And I weep in silence.

My tongue has lost its voice,
My eyes no longer see.
I see my light is fading
And my warmth is turning cold.

The world says nothing to me,
Silence is all around;
My brothers are now strangers
And solitude is my refrain.

I have looked down deep within myself
And trod the path of the spirit.
I have gazed within in terror
And seen my withering despair.

Anguish is my daily bread.
Fear set me to trembling.
The last faint vestiges of me
Dissolve and disappear.

I no longer know of love:
Have I ever known it?
I do not even seek it;
It is a hollow echo.

Look to me, my God,
Save me one more time.
Make my anguish yours
And my frailty thine.

Stop me from pronouncing
The last words of my life;
The last words raised to you:
Why have you abandoned me?

WITNESS AMONG MEN

Lord, my God and creator,
You are the Father of Jesus Christ.
You have fatherhood
Over me and my brother men.

During the life you have given me
I did proclaim your name,
And into every ear
I whispered of your love.

I have lived with human beings,
I have witnessed to your love.
And now I simply wait
For you to return in peace.

With those who wept in tears
I shed my tears of sorrow.
With those who celebrated
I sang and danced for joy.

To those who persecuted me
I brought your benediction.
To those who readied me for death
I spoke of the risen Christ.

In all the events of my life
You were present, O my Lord.
I proclaim again my trust
And confidence in your love.

We loudly proclaim your glory,
And your love in Jesus Christ.
May your Spirit open our hearts
For every age to come. Amen!

IN CHRIST'S LOVE

Nothing can separate us
From the love of Jesus Christ.
He brings us victory
Over the troubles of this life.

    Even if life brings anguish to us
    And the pangs of death,
    Even if hunger destroys our body
    And other men humiliate us,

Even if the cold pierces our flesh
And the heat sears it through,
Even if our hearts are tortured
And plunged down into death,

    Even if men pursue and dog us
    And put to death our brothers,
    Even if we find only hate
    And have to pass through fire,

All these sufferings are our glory,
We abide in Jesus Christ;
In him we find our strength
And in his love our life. Amen!

Prayers of Thanksgiving

CHRIST'S COMING

It is right and just
That we give you thanks,
God our Father.
For you did not choose
To remain away from us
And you have willed
That your love for men
Take the form of man
As God among men.

That is why you sent us
Him who from eternity
Was to come and save us,
Jesus Christ, your Son.
Through him is revealed
Your Word and also your life,
Through him is your love expressed.
Truly man and truly God,
He taught us your name.
You willed that he be our brother,
Thus revealing to us
That you are our Father.

Thus after his death
And resurrection
You willed that he be glorified
And gave him the name of Lord.
That is why in Jesus' name
All of your creation,
Inspired by your Spirit,
Praises you in joy.

HOLY THURSDAY

Toward you, our God and Father,
We raise this day
Our praise and blessing,
For the wondrous man
To whom you gave your name,
Jesus Christ, your Son.

It is he who by his life
Showed us the only road to truth.
On the eve of his death,
Which gave us victory over sin,
He left us in your name
The food that is our true salvation,
His body and his blood.
Through this bread and wine so new
We abide in communion with him,
And hence abide in you.

So on this joyous day
We remember that sacrifice
And we offer up to you
With ourselves and all creation
The body and blood of your Son.
That is why all mankind
Reunited in Jesus Christ,
Together with the whole creation
That you made for them,
Turn to you and now proclaim
That you are the holy one.
We give you thanks,
God our Father,
On this day when your Son, Jesus,
Ascended into heaven,
Stealing away from our sight
To participate in your inaccessible light.
Our eyes can no longer see him,
Our ears cannot hear the voice
That reveals your Word to us.
His disappearance creates in us
The emptiness of love.

From that day on
We await his return,
Living in hope
Of his return to us.
Since that day
We know he has already returned
And returns every day
In all our fellow men.
Because he came
We now possess true life
Which is your life;
We now know authentic love,
Your love.
Through this singular man
Whom you called back to you
When his earthly mission was fulfilled,
All men gathered in your Spirit
Join with all creation
To chant their feeling of hope
In chanting that you are holy.

ASCENSION

Our festive joy today
Rises to you, our Father.
The silence, songs and words
Are directed to you
And share in the praise
Of all creation.
You have called back to yourself
Jesus Christ, your Son,
Through whom you gave us your salvation.
He returns today
To share your glory.
In this movement
That draws him back to you,
He draws us with him
That your breath may be given
To all humanity.
And so we penetrate
Into the mystery of your Son.
Our eyes can no longer see him
But we know that his return
Has already begun;
His disappearance creates in us
The empty void of love.
But we know that by our love
We give him back his visage.
We abide in him and hence in you.
He gathers us together today
And through his Holy Spirit
Our communion proclaims your glory.

PENTECOST

It is just and right, Lord,
That we proclaim this day
Your power and your glory.
In your infinite love
You gave us your Son.
Taking us with him
In his death and resurrection
He brought us your salvation.
Today you willed in his name
To complete this work of love
And renew the face of the earth
By sending us your Spirit.
Through this Spirit,
We know that Jesus is your Son;
Through this Spirit,
We believe that he has revealed your love to us;
Through this Spirit,
We walk in awareness of your name.
Your Spirit opens our lips and tongues
That they may proclaim to all the world
That you are our Father.
Your Spirit opens our eyes
That they may see in creation
The grandeur of your glory.
Your Spirit gathers us
Into a single People,
Teaching us to sing
With the whole universe
That you are God, the holy one.

MARRIAGES

We give you thanks,
God our Father,
For above all else
You are love.

From all eternity
You have willed that men
Share in your creation
And move it toward you
In love;
Through this creative love
That comes from you
They open up to life
And draw closer to you.

OPTION I

In Jesus Christ
You have willed that this love
Be very close to us;
And that all men,
Celebrating the mystery of your Son,
Might grow in you and prepare his return
Into our humanity.

OPTION II

In Jesus Christ
Your love drew near
And we now know it.
In Jesus Christ
You give our love
Its full plenitude.
You give it its true name
Which is your own.

COMMON

That is why the impulse which reunites us
In the light of your Spirit
Is an impulse of love.
And it is your love
Which on this day
Gathers us with all creation
To proclaim and sing our joy
That you are the holy one.

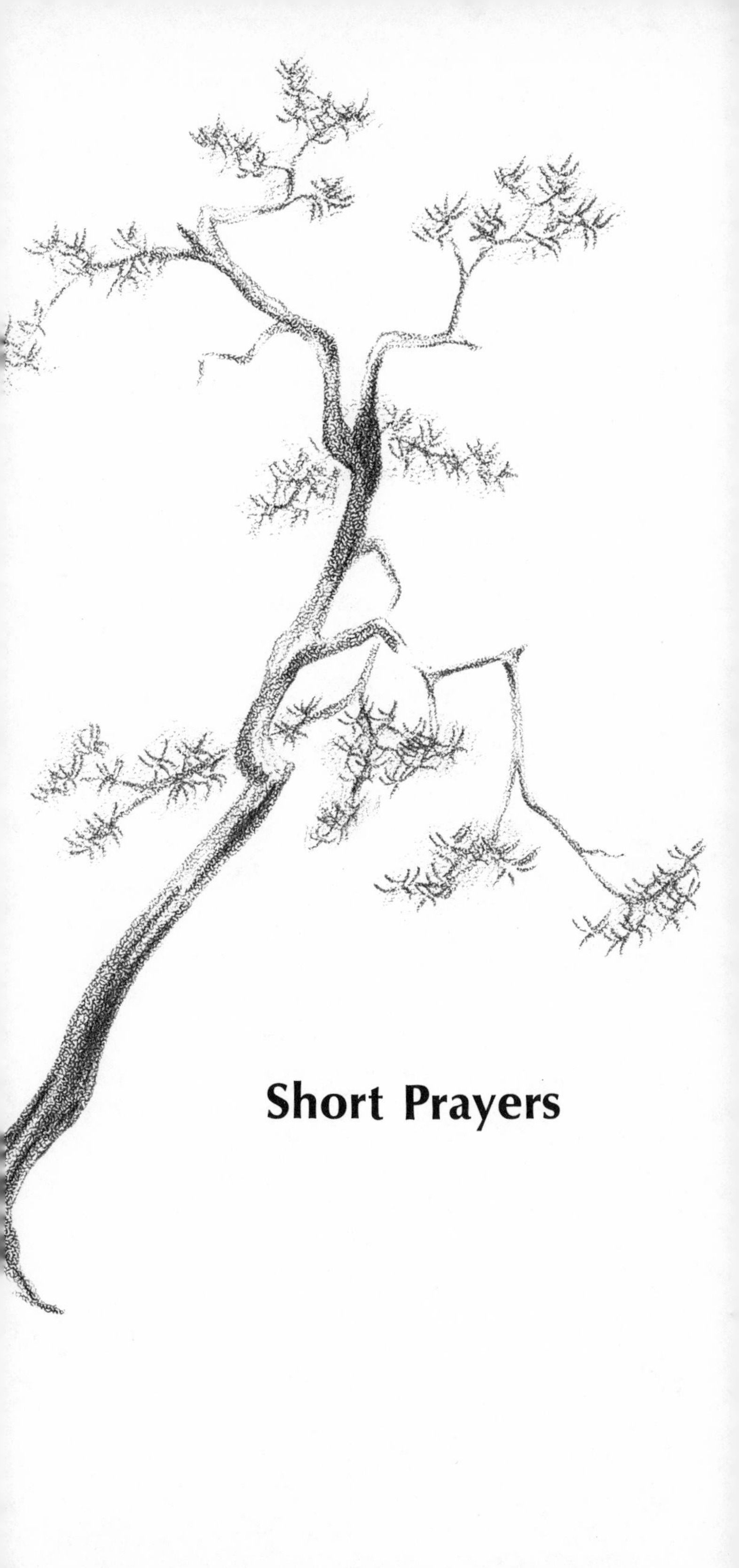

Short Prayers

1

Lord, we pray
That the prayer on our lips
May be the prayer in our hearts
In the truth of your light.

2

May your Spirit, Lord,
Enter into our lives
And help us to better understand
The mystery of your love.

3

Grant us, O Lord,
That we may hope in your mercy
Which alone can snatch us from sin.

4

Help us, O Lord,
To be instruments of justice and peace,
Bearing witness to light and truth.

5

May your Spirit inspire
The way we lead our lives
And may we be reunited one day
In an encounter with your glory.

6

Give us your peace, O Lord,
Which surpasses every treasure
And then may it lead us
To understand other men.

7

Lord, may we not turn astray
The power you give us over the universe.
May our mastery over creation
Lead man to true fulfillment.

8

Lord,
May your coming enter us
And buoy up our spirits
From darkness and from doubt.

9

Lord,
Effect in our lives
The unity of your love
In justice and in truth.

10

Lord, let nothing
Separate us from you
And let our lives
Be pointed toward you.

11

Lord, let us share in your creation
And may our love
Be, in your image,
Light and strength and truth.

12

Lord, may your name
Be on our lips
And your love in our hearts
As it was with your Son.

13

Lord, may the freedom
Won by your Son
Not be an idle word for us,
But lead us with our brothers
To knowledge of your glory.

14

Lord, may the power of your Word
Penetrate our lives
And guide them
In the search for your plenitude.

15

We pray, Lord Jesus,
Remain with us
So that with you
We may go to the Father.

16

Lord, we pray,
Help us to cast on the world
A glance of love
That will be creative.

17

Lord,
Help us to be witnesses to your love
And help large numbers of our brothers
To come to faith
Through the action of your Spirit.

18

Lord, we ask you
To illumine our lives
By sending to them
Your singular light.

19

Lord,
Through our brotherly love
May we draw closer each day
To the return of your Son.

20

Lord, may our communion
Bear witness to our brothers
That they can find therein
The image of your kingdom.

21

Lord, we pray you,
Let your Church
Be a place of unity
Bearing witness to peace and love.

22

Lord, we pray you,
Help your Church
To work for man's betterment
Through the dynamism
Of faith in your love.

23

We pray you, Lord,
Help us to respect our brothers.
Enable us to see in them
The visage of your Son.

24

We pray you, Lord,
That we may be servants of your Spirit,
In the diversity of gifts
That he has given us.

25

May your Spirit be within us
Inspiring us to pray—
He who helps us move
From lowly fear to love.

26

Help us, O Lord, to be
In communion with all men
That their pain may be our suffering
And their joy our happiness.

27

Help our love, O Lord,
To be in service to our brothers,
To seek their full awakening
In justice and in truth.

28

Help us, O Lord,
To view others with patience
And to see in them only
The good that they do.

29

Inspire our prayer, O Lord,
That it may point to you,
For you alone can know
The need we have of you.

30

Give us, O Lord,
The humility of our faith
And the discretion of our love,
For all comes from you and returns to you.

31

Lord, take away from us
Pride in the good we do
So that through us
Our brothers may see your glory.

32

Lord, we pray you,
Be the light in our night,
The inspiration behind our faith,
And the goal of our hopes.

33

Help us, O Lord,
To become new men.
Woo us from what is not of you
That we may be clothed in your light.

34

Lord, we pray you,
Help us to overcome the limits of our bodies
That they may always be the means
For an encounter with other men.

35

We pray that you will help us
To ever seek your glory
And not our own satisfaction
When we proclaim your Gospel.

36

Help us, O Lord,
Never to impose on our brothers
What is beyond their forces
By recognizing better our own frailty.

37

Help us, Lord,
To be poor in spirit
That along with you
We may possess your kingdom.

38

Help us, O Lord,
To work for peace
So that in this peace
We may find your love.

39

Help us, O Lord,
To be merciful and pardon offenses,
For we ourselves have need
Of your understanding.

Prayers for the Eucharistic Banquet

I

Father of ours,
Creator and holy God,
In Jesus Christ, your Son,
You revealed to us
Your wisdom and your strength,
Your power and your love.

You gather us together this day
To manifest to men
The splendor of your salvation,
The strength of your light,
And the glory of your name.
We ask you, Lord,
To send us your Spirit.
May he sanctify
All that we offer you:
Our lives,
Our hearts,
Our love.

In order to gather us into one body
On the eve of his passion
HE EXTENDED HIS HANDS OVER THE BREAD
AND, BLESSING THE FATHER,
BROKE IT
AND GAVE IT TO HIS DISCIPLES, SAYING:

"TAKE AND EAT.
THIS IS MY BODY DELIVERED UP FOR YOU."

IN LIKE MANNER AFTER THE REPAST
HE TOOK THE CUP OF OUR SALVATION
AND SAID:

"TAKE AND DRINK,
THIS IS MY BLOOD,
THE BLOOD OF THE NEW COVENANT
SHED FOR THE REMISSION OF SINS.
YOU WILL DO THIS
IN MEMORY OF ME."

Recalling to mind the death
And the glorious resurrection of your Son,
We believe, O Lord our God,
That he came in our flesh and blood
To bring us to new life
And to give us hope
In your coming to our midst.

May your Spirit,
God of power,
Open our hearts to your love;
May he lead us as one People
To knowledge of your wisdom.

May he reunite us in Jesus Christ,
Introduce us to your thinking
And help us to know your love.

Animated by the breath of your Spirit
We affirm our unity
With the entire Church
Spread throughout the world.
We pray for the pope
And for our bishop,
The witnesses of our union
With each and every man
Who proclaims his faith
In Jesus Christ, your Son.

Finally, Lord, look down on our assembly.
Grant that it may abide
In the same communion;
May the unity of your love
Pass into each one's life
Going beyond our sins.
This assembly knows its weakness
But it has faith in your mercy
Proclaimed in Jesus Christ
Your Son,
Our Lord.

THROUGH HIM,
GATHERED TOGETHER AROUND HIM,
UNITED IN HIS LOVE
THROUGH THE INSPIRATION OF THE SPIRIT,
WE OFFER PRAISE TO YOU
AND PROCLAIM YOUR GLORY
FOREVER AND EVER. AMEN.

II

God and Father,
Infinite love,
You are holiness itself.
You have willed that all men
Be elevated to you
And know your name.
You the one and only
Send us your Son,
The fruit of your love for us.

He, shortly before his passion
Where he conquered death
By his resurrection,
Willed to dwell with us forever
By leaving us an authentic sign
Of his presence
And your Spirit's action.

THAT IS WHY, THIS DAY,
HE TOOK BREAD AND,
BLESSING HIS FATHER, BROKE IT
AND GAVE IT TO HIS DISCIPLES, SAYING:

"TAKE AND EAT,
THIS IS MY BODY, DELIVERED UP FOR YOU."

AND WHEN THE MEAL WAS FINISHED
HE TOOK THE CUP OF SALVATION AND SAID:

"TAKE AND DRINK.
THIS IS MY BLOOD
SHED FOR YOU

TO DELIVER YOU FROM SIN
AND REVEAL TO YOU
THE LOVE OF THE FATHER FOR HIS
CHILDREN
YOU WILL DO THIS IN MEMORY OF ME."

So in celebrating the death
And glorious resurrection
Of your Son,
We profess our faith
In your existence.
We affirm that your Spirit
Is living among us
As he has and ever will
In ages yet to come.

We believe that this same Spirit
Is preparing the advent of your Son
And the final revelation of your visage
In our humanity.
We look and wait for this return,
Praying to you, holy God,
Living in your love
And proclaiming by our union
That Christ is our brother
And that we are your sons.

We render you this witness
In communion with all mankind
And your whole creation,
With all the Christian people
Touched by your love
And animated by your Spirit,
With the heads of your Church,
The pope,
Our bishop.

We do not separate our prayer
From the human beings you have called to you
Who have passed through the road of death
And thus have the revelation of your being
And the blessed vision of your glory.

Finally, Lord God,
We ask you to see in our assembly
The true and profound unity
Of all those who believe that you are God.
They are preparing your coming
And they know that
Your love and mercy
Revealed through your Son, Jesus Christ,
Encompass their sins.

THROUGH HIM,
GATHERED TOGETHER AROUND HIM,
UNITED IN HIS LOVE
THROUGH THE INSPIRATION OF THE SPIRIT,
WE OFFER PRAISE TO YOU
AND PROCLAIM YOUR GLORY
FOREVER AND EVER. AMEN.

Sample Office

FIRST READING

Beloved,
Let us love one another
Since love is from God
And whoever loves
Is born of God and knows God.
He who does not love has never known God
For God is love.

R. Let us love one another
Since love is from God.

V. He who does not love has never known God
For God is love.
Whoever loves is born of God.
He is called a son of God.

SECOND READING

In this was the love of God
Made manifest to us:
God sent his only Son into the world
That we might live through him.
This is what his love implies:
It was not we who loved our God
But he who showed his love for us,
Who sent his Son as victim
To atone for all our sins.

R. Let us love . . .

V. In this was love made manifest:
God so loved the world
He gave his only Son
To deliver us from death.

THIRD READING

Through this we recognize
That we abide in him
And he in us:
In that he gave us his Spirit.
And we have seen and
Do attest
That the Father sent his Son,
The Savior of the world.
If a person proclaims that Jesus
Is the Son of God,
God abides in him
And he in God.
And we, we have acknowledged
The love God has for us
And we believe in it.
God is love:
If a person abides in love,
He abides in God and God in him.

R. Let us love . . .

V. And we, we have acknowledged
The love God has for us
And we believe in it.
He gave us his own Spirit.

FOURTH READING

As for us, let us love,
Since he has loved us first.
No one has ever seen our God.
But if we love one another
God abides in us
And his love is fulfilled in us.
If someone says: "I love God"
And hates his brother,
He is a liar:
If he does not love the brother he sees,
How can he love the God he does not see?
That is the commandment
Which we have received from him:
That he who loves God
Also loves his brother.

R. Let us love . . .

V. No one has seen God.
In Jesus we come to know him.
He remains present among us
In the love we have for our brothers.